AF614172

Tales of Trees

Sue Johnson & Bob Woodroofe

Greenwood Press

First published in 2004
Revised & republished 2018

Greenwood Press
38 Birch Avenue
Evesham
Worcs WR11 1YJ

Tel 01386 446477

http://greenwoodpress.co.uk

Many of these poems have previously been published in various poetry magazines and performed at readings

Front cover illustration
Sue Johnson

ISBN-0-9521165-3-7

ISBN 978-0-9521165-3-0

Introduction

We talked about creating this collection ever since we first met based on our different backgrounds and perspectives on life.

These paired poems are derived from our family trees that shaped the landscapes we grew up in.

Sue was born in Orpington, Kent and is a poet, short storywriter & novelist She is interested in the benefits of creativity to health.

Bob was born and bred in Evesham, Worcestershire. Originally trained as a scientist, he is a poet with a keen interest in nature & the environment and is intrigued by the cross over between science and art.

Dedication

This book is dedicated to both our families,
the inspiration for the poems.

It is especially in memory of our fathers although
they never met except through us.

Frederick Stephen Bloss
15th March 1923 to 8th August 2003

&

Arthur Woodroofe (Woody)
22nd May 1918 to 22nd September 1979

Contents

1 Music maps
2 So they say
3 Girls don't drive
4 Angle
5 Incantations
6 Thirteens
7 Hideout
8 El Consuelo
9 Herne Bay
10 Revolve
11 Highway of dreams
12 Stamping Ground
13 Chislehurst Caves
14 Below the surface
15 Geography
16 Cauldron
17 1968 remembered
18 Trowman
19 Churchyard
20 Headstones
21 29.03.2001
22 Ballycanew
23 Daisies
24 Avoca Blue
25 Sunflowers
26 Hoarder
27 Rose for remembrance
28 Meeting

Music Maps

when I was three I went to bed before The Archers
started on the radiogram

in the afternoons there was Listen With Mother
my brother and I sat together in the big armchair
with pink roses on the cover

we went to stay at somebody's house.
I don't remember who the people were but I see
morning light coming through a kitchen window
onto a blue and white striped jug and hear a radio
playing a song 'South of the Border Down Mexico
Way'

I didn't know where Mexico was but I had a vision
of a wide dusty road lined with trees and passing
through the avenue in an open topped car

So they say

whilst being washed fell off the draining board
head first into a bucket of persil water
knocked all the heads off the tulips
in the garden with a stick
climbed the garden wall and was away down the road
till someone brought me back
stood on the front gate and threw a stone
smashed a passing car's windscreen
cut my head on the gate then hid
in the outside loo before passing out
scrumped apples and hid them up my jumper
before bringing them home to eat
threw spanners and turned the air blue
in the back yard when the bike wouldn't mend

or so they say

Girls don’t drive

Girls don’t drive trains he says as his feet
barricade me at one end of the dark
enclosed space. It is too wet to go outside
so we play in the bottom of Gran’s dresser.
The stuffy air carries the smell of cake tins.
They make a metal mountain in the rocking
chair by the rain lashed window.

In our hideout we conjure up the coal scent
of tunnels on our way to Edinburgh.
Its the usual place and we always go at night.
The smell of steam trains reminds me of Grandad
and I want to be him driving over the viaduct.
Today I have to be fireman again. Orpington
to Edinburgh is a long way to stoke an engine.

I am desperate to take my turn on the footplate
watch the rails through the grimy window
as they stretch into the next dark tunnel.
We argue; scuffle in confined darkness.
Heads collide. The door bursts open.
We tumble, snapping and snarling
into the world where girls don’t drive trains.

Angle

wade through grass scuff shine from shoes
acid suck of sorrel moistens dry mouth
pick a way across bog from tuft to tuft
past the pump graveyard from school cross-country

to the rivulet that teems with loach and minnow
on to the damp depression that marks the pond where
orange bellied monsters roam through tangled weed
to common's meandering stream guarded by creaking willows

strained to the winds tune thighs of mossy trunks split and fallen
lean over choked pools beneath whose scummed surface
spotted and barred pike lurk fin the water waiting ease through
spears of fringing reed freeze to moorhens loud 'kurruck'

silently curse as it skitters away the black ooze clings
draws sulphide into air climb up inch out along branch
rasp of bark and lichen against skin scratches
clamped legs till they reach the cool of mossy patch

notch the elder arrow onto string of garden twine
draw back the willow bow the trembling hand releases
thin shaft pierces sallow light calm water explodes boils
wished that we had hit knew we were wide of the mark

Incantations

"I'll cut your north ear off if you misbehave."
Shuffling of feet. Trying to work out
which ear to protect.

She chased Roger with the copper tongs
because he wouldn't wash his neck.
She has eyes in the back of her head.
Her bottom's the size of Margate my Dad says.

She goes to church every Sunday but everyone
knows its a front for other activities.

She has a strange thing on her dressing table
with long pins in it.
She says they're for keeping her hat on straight

but we know

they're for impaling children who are bad.

My cousin Nicky saw her do it once
and he knows everything.

She won the last war single-handed.
Hitler would have been too scared to come here.

She mutters incantations under her breath
about juvenile delinquents.
The words taste to me like that white stuff
she drinks every night
that is her special magic spell.

Thirteens

they stood
rooted in the shed
long after being worn
bindweed strained to climb
their smooth sides
but failed
lay in tangled mass
over insteps
tripping them up
earth still clings
to worn soles
where had they been
on their last journey
garden - lane - fields
why were they left here
to languish in the dark

Hideout

they enter the wooden shell
creep into green darkness
through the curtains of ivy

sitting in a circle on the mud floor
they share black jacks
flying saucers liquorice coils

two squabble all suck loudly
they watch as he shakes
the matchbox

then he takes out a match
grinning as bone-white faces stare
for a moment there is silence
as he strikes it on the box

his fingers burn he lets go
flames dance on rough wood
a golden fountain soars
and crackles sparks fly

screams and running feet echo
as the old greenhouse dies
to ashes and charred ivy fingers

El consuelo de luxe Bahana - Kingston, Jamaica

flamboyant boxes
ornate reds – golds - silver
inside sleek tubes
blunt nosed rockets
empty of tight rolled contents
only the smell remains

used the biggest
unscrewed the cap
split cardboard cases
poured black powder in
drilled a hole inserted the fuse
carried outside

buried down side of house
in the flower bed
against the wall
lit it darted back
round the corner
held our breath

a muffled crump
peered round corner
saw house wall
mud splattered, powder streaked,
and from the crater
a final whiff of smoke curl

Herne Bay

Shingle crunches under my unwilling feet
and I wonder why we always visit in winter
when there is no ice cream, no tea trays
and the beach huts are closed.
Grandma jokes about the wind coming "straight from Siberia"
as we watch the hostile grey sea.

Later, Auntie Nell answers the door, her brown eyes hard as bullets.
The dingy hallway smells of boiled cabbage and urine stained sheets.
Auntie Nell looks after Miss Howard who is 100 years old.
My father asks what Miss Howard's husband did
and she looks at him with milky blue eyes and says
"My dear, I was never a married lady."

Auntie Nell smells the lunchtime gin on Grandma's breath
and sniffs disapprovingly as she puts the kettle on.
She makes tea with sour cream lumps in it
and takes something green and mouldy out of a cake tin.

Grandma spots a brandy bottle and says: "Shall we have a drink, Nell?"
Nell, who is teetotal says: "It's for medicinal purposes only."
"I don't feel at all well,"says Grandma. While they argue,
my brother and I smuggle mouldy cake into Mum's handbag

When the washing up is done, Nell leads us into the front room
with its half drawn curtains and shrine to her husband Fred,
who was killed on the day the Armistice was signed.

We look at his uniform in the glass case
and Grandma causes another argument by saying
we should drink a toast to our glorious dead
and the cold grey sea keeps up its endless rhythm.

Revolve

quiet now it gathers dust bulking the room
hand built feet forged in iron bolted to the floor
still the old belt hisses to the treadle
that pushes against you resists your weight
hand wheels cold to touch rotate smoothly

the cast wheel hums to the task the pulley
loose on the drive shaft rattles emptily needs oil
the turret slides at constant speed over the bed
but tool-less now the hardened carbon steels
lie racked in wait silver sharpness dulled to grey

the chuck gapes hungrily for the next work piece
what of those shaped and turned over the years
the oversize bearing from solid phosphor bronze
carefully reamed to one thousandth of an inch
the cake stand that spun in almost perpetual motion

does the piston with skirt machined to balance
its twin still pump in the heart of the BSA
the stamped initials on the heavy wooden box
full of cogs and gears whose meshed precision
altered the rate of spindle rotation varied the pitch

I stand here now as they did before hold the controls
pedal see the hypnotic curl of steel sliver grow
into razor coils smell the oil milking the heat
turn once more its measured length
that cuts the constant thread of time

Highway of dreams

sometimes our street was the great Silk Road
a sultry desert scented with sandalwood
and spices where camels shimmered
in midday heat laden with bundles
of rich fabric coloured turquoise
purple crimson and gold
that were really Mum's second best
curtains and an old wedding veil

in winter it was Antarctica and I was
Captain Scott with a mission to discover
the South Pole dressed in my brother's
balaclava and Dad's old leather gloves
I made an igloo and created a slide
just like the Cresta Run
that made the weird man from the corner house
skid dramatically on his old black boneshaker bicycle

once in my role as tight-rope walker
I tripped on the wobbly bit of wall
by the telegraph pole and fell
many feet to the circus ring below
which was next door's geranium bed

as shadows lengthened I climbed
to the look-out post in the cleft
of the lightning tree
and watched the sun sink
towards bloodstained horizon

I listened to the noise of blue and yellow parrots
as I pretended to be a bat a monkey a lemur
or a leopard ready for the kill

Stamping ground

just another crop we grew here
like the orchard where we scrumped worcesters
the strawberry field we raided the rhubarb patch
where we secretly sucked the sharp pink stems
and the plums galore all in season

we knew every field hedge birds nest
'three tree corner' the 'pigway' complete with sty
where the pig munched on sprays of elm
willows for bows elder for arrows
strings of bird scarers for explosives

rolled a dumped tyre down 'Blaney's lane'
hit a car hid when the driver chased us
dropped stones down the well long seconds
one – two – three – four – five - splash
pennies on the line for the LMS to squash

tried to ride cows enticed with grass
climbed on from the gate quickly thrown
sledged into sprout fields crashed into stems
slid wildly across flood meadows dragging feet
to stop before we reached thin ice near the river

we knew every pond and stream
for frogspawn loach and minnow
the river for perch chub and pike
fishing by touch in dead of night
writhing eels torched on the bank

plop of vole skitter of water hen
owls screech across misted fields
de Montfort's ghosts remain
haunting 'Dead Man's Ait'
just as ours will one day

Chislehurst caves

You don't remember the dripping darkness
and the icy chill of the rocks
the lanterns we carried and the faint smell
of kerosene; the way sounds echoed
from places and people we couldn't see.

You don't remember how the guide told us
there was a town here in the war.
He showed us the pitch markings
on the white rock, the chapel
and the hospital hidden underground.

You don't remember the layers of history;
how Romans, Saxons and Druids
peopled these tunnels. In the haunted cave
they took away the lanterns
and I felt a ghost breathe on me.

You don't remember the spooky stories
the guide told us and how Auntie
was angry and told him not to frighten kids.
That night you had bad dreams and screamed
about the Druids following you.

Today I tell your daughter the stories
of the caves. She laughs at the idea of ghosts
and of you being frightened by Druids.
She laughs even louder when I tell her
it was a long time ago and you don't remember.

Below the surface*

behind the brick wall the vague circular shape
surrounded by horse chestnut and sycamore
the levelled lawn betrays nothing
only the house bears the name

slip between the bars prised apart
so you can just squeeze through
the fry scatter from the warm shallows
skaters dimple the film whirligigs spin patterns
on the upside down world of the boatmen
shrimps endlessly circle and scurry

passengers and driver slake their thirst in the inn
first port of call on the dusty road into town
under the tall elm shade the horses
freed from the shafts stamp and switch their tails
lap cool water and graze the fresh grass
the glistening sweat drying on their trembling sides

** All that remains of the watering pond for the coaching inn, now a private house, on the Birmingham road out of Evesham.*

Geography

lost in colour
lost in the middle of the map
with a river that goes uphill

and Mr Harding won't tell me
what I'm doing wrong

he's set himself up as a map master
controller of the world
and there's a dragon caretaker
who lives in the broom cupboard
and doesn't take care of anything

in my mind when I look at a map
that's where I always find myself
stuck in the middle of brown contour lines
in Room 4C

Cauldron

under the bench slip open
the two doors insert the next
into the glass beaker
the biggest we could find

we all took our turn
at random experimentation
added a different chemical
to see what we could concoct

Once the doors blew open
covered us in a purple cloud
eyes streaming screaming
till treated in hospital

later we exhibited
the pockmarked cheek

1968 remembered

the colour of orange pumpkins
reminds me of Hallowe'en
and the lipstick Lesley bought me
for my fourteenth birthday and how
I was never confident enough to wear it

that was the year I wore a black kaftan
decorated with gold embroidery
with silver earrings (the only pair
I ever owned) and sandals that hurt
but I didn't want to prove my Mum right
by saying so. I played Scott Mackenzie's
record all day long and wanted to go
to San Francisco to be a flower child

I remember how my Dad worried
about drugs and boys and why
I didn't wear pretty dresses any more

seeing the pumpkins against a dark sky
I remember how my first teacher said
the sky should always be painted blue
but I know life was never like that

Trowman*

you strode bank and deck rode the carryall of the stream
stowed the cargo one hundred tons stone salt metal tools

plied the swirling flow breasted queen's heavy glide
nosed upstream with sturgeon royal - twaite and allis shad

past the putcheon waist deep in tide
fine tuned to the flood waiting homing silver's touch

slipped sheets of elvers twixt punt and coracle
shooting long nets for the king of fish

shallow draughted float over shoal and ketch
in wave crammed funnel mouth ride out the foaming bore

when square sail went you bow hauled upstream
then barged behind the tug were overhauled by steam

heard red brindled cow low through butter haze
the drum of snipe echo along meadow sluices

caught the blades sunflash that mows the hay
clash of binder that breaks the calm of flowered ham

drank the music of the reeds followed at twenty-one past
deep scour of red marl cliff followed Sabrina's course to sea

** Some of my ancestors were bargees on the river Severn, one was lost overboard.*

Churchyard

a new gate replaces the one
children used to swing on
it is overhung with hawthorn
and Grandma was angry
when I took the creamy
soap smelling blossoms indoors
white flowers are unlucky she said
as she threw them from the window

why didn't she uproot
the cow parsley
from the edges of the lane
and repaint the roses
in the ornamental beds
like Alice in Wonderland's
Queen of Hearts

wandering amongst lichened
headstones uneven as teeth
I notice white bluebells
growing on her grave

Headstones

the drive a winding path bramble overhung
through rusted gates cow parsley showers
speckled wood shies in dappled light
then spirals madly into sky
starlings bustle through grass tufts
between graves lain under flowering thorn
hooded jackdaw watches from the tower

under the church clock bluebells strike the hours
nourish a small tortoiseshell's sweet appetite
blown beech bud sheathes pile the path
a cuckoo calls both notes clear and true
orange tips seek 'jack by the hedge'
yew's flaked red flavoured bark
shelters in its own deep shade

flowers butterflies birds trees
all these I name
spirits of life among the dead
like the names carved on stone
they mean nothing unless known and
each has grown its own association
particular to me

29.3.2001

I will remember the flooded fields seen from the train
and how a shaft of sudden sunlight made
the reflections dance and lit the distant hills

I will remember hiding from showers in tiny shops
emerging with arms laden,
the friendliness of the woman in the cafe
and the taste of coffee and hot rolls

I will remember how you loved the daffodils and anemones
in the Cathedral gardens.
We talked about the flowers and, for today, left unspoken
the fears about your failing sight

I will remember how you took photos of the exotic hats
all ready for Ascot and we laughed
because the snooty shop assistant
thought you were a rich American

I will remember the trendy shop
that sold the sort of clothes you hated
me to wear when I was sixteen
and how you insisted on buying me
a blue tie dyed t-shirt with stars on

I don’t want to remember the lump in my throat
as we said goodbye.
I kissed you and watched you walk away
then stood weeping on the bridge
as your train left the station

Ballycanew*

under a stained glass window the vault's
spiked railings rust with time

nature reclaims ferns
spring from damp corners
lichens creep over stone coats
obliterate their epitaphs

did they come out of the river mists
march under an orange flag
to the beat of a Boyne drum

the written record
by reverend pen impressed
lost in the rebellion as the registers burned

swallows trace their tales
on white pages floating in blue
the sun is hot on the face
the stones warm to touch

they lie within generations collected here
never knowing me that I would come

to pay homage to dig down
amongst my roots unearthing theirs

** A small village in Co. Wexford, Ireland*
to where I traced some of my ancestors.

Daisies

White daisies star the lawn
in the cloister gardens
and I remember how my friend Jane and I
once spent a summer afternoon
making a daisy chain that nearly
stretched along the garden fence
until my brother came
and tore it to shreds.

White is the colour of mourning in India.

White feathers were given to
conscientious objectors in the First World War.

My Gran said if you found a
small white feather
in an unexpected place
it meant an angel had come visiting.

Today I find a white feather
in the middle of a daisy ring.
I pick it up and make a wish
place its softness in the cupped shape
of a hollyhock leaf and remember
how the feel of their leaves
always reminds me of the blankets
on my bed at Gran's house.

Avoca blue*

when I found you one in a warehouse full
your colours swirled blue sea white cloud
blended into brown earth green forest
around your town the river runs through

a moment then seen from space
I wonder when no other quite the same
painted by hand SF white initials
scratched Susanna Fawsitt

did she care where you would go
on what shelf stand who would
hold you in palm of hand
do you continue family tradition

did mine eat and drink
fill theirs with flowers
you carry her name into the future
yet hold so much of my past

** range of pottery depicting the Earth , as seen from space, designed and made in county Wicklow, Ireland.*

Sunflowers

when you are gone
I will remember the sunflowers

the plaque made by patients
and their teacher
in the day centre

the bunch in a vase in the room
where we made the film of the hospice
the three of us sitting
under a huge mobile of turquoise fish
and lilac seahorses

Mum said the sunflowers
looked like the faces
of a mother with a cluster of children round her

later in the canteen we saw a man
taking sunflowers to his wife

I will remember your face
lit up like a sunflower
when we collected you
from the garden pavilion

I tell you about the fields of sunflowers in Italy
and how I will see them and you
again one day

Hoarder

you could only just edge round the door lose yourself
in the maze the accumulation of ages piled
head high with narrow corridors between

wreaths of blue smoke hung under the anglepoise lamp
that hovered over the workbench in its shaft of light they
wafted with the cough that punched a hole through the haze

He was hunched over the workbench engrossed
in his latest creation I call it that creation because
they weren't conventional but they always did the job

from pieces of metal wood plastic he would fashion
whatever was required no drawing he just created it

in his warren he knew where everything was he could
lay his hands on it given time for thought all those
things that lay undisturbed for years after they
disappeared into the maw of his cave with the words
'Don't throw that away it'll come in useful sometime'

the room is empty now bare boards rise up
freed from the weight they carried contents spread
around families passed on to future generations

In front of where the workbench used to be there is
a worn patch on the floorboards and somewhere
hanging in the air a hint of woodbine

Rose for remembrance

on the last Sunday I saw you we kissed goodbye
and told each other ‘I love you’

eyes blurred with tears
I went to the chapel and lit a candle for you

picked a red rose from the wall
outside the hospice and pressed it in my notebook

on Wednesday night I had a dream about you
when we walked a shimmering landscape

you said you knew where you had to go
but would I help you find the door

we searched but did not find it
and you were agitated

then on Friday morning when the phone rang early
I knew you’d found the door you were looking for

Meeting*

we meet at last you and I
you Avonmore and Avonbeg
meeting here for time immemorial
waters mingling into Avoca

I from another Avon's side
have journeyed here to see you
you prompt me to write in response
as Moore did all those years ago

rippling waters fringed with willow
mallard loaf and preen on shingle bars
wagtail feeds her chicks under the bank
birdsong answers your chattering call

I too have answered I have come
another river wells inside me
to be here by your side at last
where my people once stood

the scene now changed
your tree reduced to a stump
banks encased in concrete
tourists call snap and go

but still the spirits linger on
Moore and my people you and I
all of us in our own time
like the bright waters meeting

**The Meeting of the waters' , a poem by Thomas Moore, his tree can still be seen at Avoca, Co. Wicklow, Ireland.*

About the Authors

Sue Johnson is a poet, short story writer & novelist. Her other interests include reading, walking & yoga. Sue is a Writing Magazine Creative Writing Tutor & also runs her own brand of writing workshops.

Born & bred & still living in the Vale of Evesham Bob Woodroofe's poems appear in many poetry magazines & are performed locally. Inspired by the natural world, the landscape & local tradition he attempts to bring the magic of nature & its restorative & healing qualities to a wider audience.

Also available from the

Greenwood Press
38 Birch Avenue
Evesham
Worcs. WR11 1YJ

website http://greenwoodpress.co.uk

e-mail info@greenwoodpress.co.uk

by Bob Woodroofe

A trilogy of poetry collections from
life & nature in the Vale of Evesham

Nature, Reflections & Spirit of the Vale

In search of greenness

Something Stirred

***t**he Poetry Collection*

Pick of the crop

Joint poetry collections by
Sue Johnson & Bob Woodroofe

Tales of Trees** & **Journey

Creative Writing books
by Sue Johnson

Writer's Toolkit
&
Writer's Toolkit 2, 3 & 4

www.ingramcontent.com/pod-product-compliance
Ingram Content Group UK Ltd.
Pitfield, Milton Keynes, MK11 3LW, UK
UKHW041643190726
13854UKWH00006B/2669

9 780952 116530